Scalping Trading Top 5 Strategies:

Making Money WITH

The Ultimate Guide to Fast Trading in Forex and Options

© **Copyright 2016 - All rights reserved.**

In no way is it legal to reproduce, duplicate, or transmit any part of this document in either electronic means or in printed format. Recording of this publication is strictly prohibited and any storage of this document is not allowed unless with written permission from the publisher. All rights reserved.

The information provided herein is stated to be truthful and consistent, in that any liability, in terms of inattention or otherwise, by any usage or abuse of any policies, processes, or directions contained within is the solitary and utter responsibility of the recipient reader. Under no circumstances will any legal responsibility or blame be held against the publisher for any reparation, damages, or monetary loss due to the information herein, either directly or indirectly.

Respective authors own all copyrights not held by the publisher.

Legal Notice:

This book is copyright protected. This is only for personal use. You cannot amend, distribute, sell, use, quote or paraphrase any part or the content within this book without the consent of the author or copyright owner. Legal action will be pursued if this is breached.

Disclaimer Notice:

Please note the information contained within this document is for educational and entertainment purposes only. Every attempt has been made to provide accurate, up to date and reliable complete information. No warranties of any kind are expressed or implied. Readers acknowledge that the author is not engaging in the rendering of legal, financial, medical or professional advice.

By reading this document, the reader agrees that under no circumstances are we responsible for any losses, direct or indirect, which are incurred as a result of the use of information contained within this document, including, but not limited to, —errors, omissions, or inaccuracies.

Table of Contents

Introduction 1

Chapter 1: About Forex 6

Chapter 2: One-Minute Strategy 8

Chapter 3: Meta Scalper 15

Chapter 4: MACD Indicator 24

Chapter 5: Short Momentum Scalper 34

Chapter 6: About Options 41

Chapter 7: Gamma Scalping 43

Conclusion 53

Glossary 54

Introduction

Scalping refers to the fast-paced trading strategy where investors use small price changes in the market to produce several small profits, which then quickly compound into larger ones. Typically, a scalper will place several trades during the day, ranging anywhere from five to ten, to 200 or more. The belief behind this strategy is that making several smaller trades minimizes the risk of major losses, while still guaranteeing a profit in the end. This technique of scalping the market, combined with strict exit strategies that are used to prevent losses, can further increase scalpers potential to gain profit from their trading efforts.

Scalping can accomplished in two different ways: through manual efforts, or automated systems. Manual scalping requires a person who is educated on the technique to scan for signals in the market that suggest when to conduct rapid buy and sell procedures. They operate with the goal of maximizing profits and minimizing losses. Automated scalping systems rely on a multitude of signals derived from technical analysis charting tools and indicators, which inform the system as to when it should buy or sell stock. These systems are programmed by manual scalpers, can use any number of strategies to successfully scalp the market automatically, and eliminate a lot of the time consuming aspect that scalping involves, while still turning profits. It is said, however, that automatic systems can eliminate some of the accuracy of the trades, as even the most advanced one can still make mistakes that a trained human eye might have otherwise avoided.

As with any investment strategy, scalping has its pros and cons. When done properly by an experienced trader, the risks are minimal and the losses can generally be avoided. With a little time and practice, anyone can develop their experience in this technique, and there are some simple strategies that can reduce the amount of risk exposure on beginning scalpers which I will discuss throughout this book. Before we get into that, though, I want to cover the pros and cons associated with this technique:

- **_Pros_**
    - Each trade is opened and closed in a very short period of time, thus greatly reducing the risk caused from exposure. The chances of reversals and losing your trading position are much less than they would be on trades that are open for longer periods of time.
    - You aren't required to be as patient as you need to be with other trading techniques, as each trade is completed in the window of a one-minute chart or a five-minute chart. Sometimes fifteen-minute charts are used, but typically scalping is restricted to smaller time intervals. (We won't be discussing anything longer than five minute charts in this book.)
    - Knowledge regarding long-term trading strategies is irrelevant, and you aren't required to have any extensive background in trading. For

experienced traders who are used to the market, this may be a drawback as your existing skills may not apply when it comes to scalping. However, you may be pleased to know that the skills that do come with scalping can be incredibly simple to master, even more so if you already have a general idea as to how the market works.

- There is an average risk-to-reward ratio of 1:1 meaning that scalping strategies can obtain higher strike rates, as opposed to a higher reward rate. While this may not sound desirable to the untrained ear, what this actually means is that the risk of incurring great losses is extremely low with this strategy.

- Automated systems can be taught to use your favourite strategies and complete the task of scalping for you. This eliminates the time spent manually performing trades, while still carrying the benefit of any profit associated with scalping. Plus, you can customize the system to use any strategy you prefer, meaning you can test a strategy and ensure it has a high success rate before applying it to your automated system.

- ***Cons***
  - Scalping may not be allowed by your preferred brokers platform, as not all brokers allow them. Here, we will discuss Forex and Options, which are both excellent scalping platforms.
  - A good trade yield will generally only carry a 1:1 risk to reward ratio, meaning that one loss could potentially deplete the gains of several successful trades. While there are strategies you can use to minimize this risk, it does still exist.
  - Pip yields are typically 5 pips or less, so many times you will have to make several trades per day in order to accomplish your financial goals. (This is where an automated system could be beneficial.)

When done right, scalping can be an incredible trading techniques to help maximize your profits in a slow, yet consistent way. There are several unique strategies that can be implemented, five of which we will discuss here, that can enormously increase your likelihood at succeeding with this technique. Plus: the strategies shared here are extremely simple to understand, and can be mastered by anyone. When done properly, scalping can enhance your income and carry you closer to the financial freedom you deserve.

Chapter 1: About Forex

Forex trading is done in the foreign exchange market. This market is generally called Forex, FX or the currency market. Forex is a globally dispersed market that is widely used for trading different currencies. Forex includes all aspects of buying, selling and exchanging various currencies at current or predetermined prices. This foreign exchange market is the largest market in the world when it comes to the volume of trades being made.

Scalping in the forex market requires you to use a real-time analysis to conduct currency trades to produce your profit. The massive size of this market makes it an incredible place to practice and execute scalping strategies. In this section, I have outlined four of the best strategies you can use for scalping the forex market. These methods have been tested and proven, and are excellent strategies for anyone who is looking to scalp: experienced or not.

Chapter 2: One-Minute Strategy

The One-Minute strategy is an excellent strategy for those looking to gain experience in the market, or for those who are just beginning to use the scalping method of trading. This method is incredibly simple to master, and each trade only requires a few seconds to complete. As the name would suggest, the One-Minute strategy uses one minute (M1) time charts to conduct each trade, which makes it quick and easy to gain profits. Although each trade is completed in such a short amount of time, it is worth noting that this strategy will require you to devote a few hours every day to concentrating solely on your trades in order to produce the profits you desire. This means that you will be required to spend a significant amount of time monitoring your trading devices, whether they be a computer, smart phone, tablet, or any combination of the above. One-Minute method trades are one of the most basic scalping strategies available, and are a wonderful place to begin if you're new to scalping. They're also an excellent strategy for those with experience, as they are simple and produce rapid profit.

It is best to utilize this strategy when the market is at its highest volatility, which is typically around the time that the New York market closes and the London market opens. Each trade will require you to complete a long order when a specific set of conditions are met, gain a few pips, and then close your position with a short order at exactly the right time. It is imperative that each step be completed when the conditions are right in order to avoid sustaining any losses to your profit.

The main element when using the One-Minute method is quantity. It is not unusual to place more than 100 trades each day in order to reach your desired daily income. Due to the nature of this strategy, you won't obtain any high gains or high losses from your trades, which translates to a much lower risk factor than you may endure with traditional trading strategies.

Indicators Used:

For this method, you will be using two different sets of indicators. The first indicator you will use is the "Exponential Moving Average" (EMA), which you will have set at a period of 50 and a period of 100. Second, you will use the Stochastic Oscillator. This one you will have set at the periods of 5, 3 and 3. It is important that you set these indicators properly and keep a close eye on them, as they are critical signals that will cue when you open a long (purchase) order and when you open a short (sell) order.

Long Order (Purchasing) Entry Overview:

Long order entry positions must be completed when the market reaches ideal conditions. For opening a long order, you will want to see your EMA's align properly. The 50 period EMA should rise above the 100 period EMA before you consider opening a long order. In addition, you want to see the Stochastic Oscillator to cross above the 20 level from below, meaning the market is coming back up from an oversold market. As soon as these conditions are met, it is safe to open your long order form.

Short Order (Selling) Entry Overview:

Short order entry positions almost always require conditions that are exactly opposite than you require in long order entry positions. For this strategy, before you place your short order, you will want to see the 50 period EMA below the 100 period EMA, and your Stochastic Oscillator should fall below the 80 (overbought) level from above. Once you see these signals, you can enter the market with your short orders.

Step By Step Instructions:

1. You will start by setting your Chart Time to 1 minute. It is also a good idea for you to open a secondary chart that is set to a 5 minute time frame so you can assess market trends and notice any signals that may pop up.
2. Next you will want to make sure you have applied the following default MetaTrader 4 indicators to your chart in the proper periods:
    - Exponential Moving Average (EMA) using the periods of 50 and 100. To increase how easy this method is, you can even give your EMA lines different colors so they're easier to tell apart during the trading process.

- Stochastic Oscillator using the periods of 5, 3 and 3.
3. You can set your currency pair to be anything you desire, however, it is recommended to use this strategy with major currency pairs if you're just starting. This is because they have the lowest available spreads which makes it easier to use.
4. To place long order (purchasing) forms:
    - Your 50 period EMA indicator should surpass your 100 period EMA indicator (so, the 50 EMA indicator should rise above the 100 EMA indicator)
    - The price at which you plan to fill your orders is close to the EMA indicators
    - The Stochastic Oscillator rises above the 20 level, from below, and is facing upwards.
5. To place short order (selling) forms:
    - The 100 EMA indicator should exceed the 50 EMA indicator (so, the 50 EMA indicator should be below the 100 EMA indicator)
    - When the spot rate is close to your EMA indicator lines
    - The Stochastic Oscillator falls below the 80 level from above, and is facing downwards.

Tips

- This scalping method is most effective if it is implemented during times when the market is at its highest volatility. As mentioned above, these periods are typically around the time when the New York market is closing, and the London market is opening.

- When scalping, it can be extremely beneficial to consult a second chart containing a longer time frame during your trades. These secondary charts are useful in providing more detailed information to the current market conditions, giving you a better idea as to when you should time your market entry positions.

- If you use MetaTrader 4 with your Forex program, there is a tool you may consider using which can expedite order placement by implementing a 1-click trading tool.

- Once you have developed and improved this strategy for yourself, and have enhanced your ability to consistently succeed with it, you may consider automating the strategy for yourself. This will save you a significant amount of time and energy, as all of your trades will be done automatically and you won't be required to manually conduct each one.

Chapter 3: Meta Scalper

The Meta Scalper strategy is an excellent scalping technique for those who have gained a little bit of experience with scalping. It relies on traders entering and exiting trades on short waves that take place when the market reaches peak overbought and oversold states. This strategy can be utilized in any market, but it is ideal to use it when the market is range bound as this minimizes the risk. While the Meta Scalper is a low yielding strategy, it still has the ability to make traders a steady profit, as it produces small yet consistent results when correctly applied.

This strategy is best used in one-minute and five-minute time frames, though it can be adjusted to work on larger ones if you desire. The Meta Scalper relies on indicator triggers as well as price behaviour at each bar (candle) to determine where the best entry positions are for each long order and short order form. It is important that you spread the risk across several trades, which will ultimately create the scalping sequence. This "averaging out" technique is essential in restricting drawdowns and creating cumulative profits. Due to its exposure across multiple trades, the impact of drawdowns on the accounts balance is limited. While many scalping strategies will abandon a trade if it enters a period of loss, this one allows for drawdowns and losses. In fact, it actually requires trades to enter a loss, so it is not advisable to use this method with aggressive leverage.

Indicators Used:

There is only one indicator used in this strategy: the Bollinger band lines. This indicator can be a bit confusing to the untrained eye, so I will take a minute to explain it to you.

The Bollinger band lines are comprised of three separate indicators, which are used to help gain a variety of information on the current state of the market. These indicators help to convey the market trend, volatility, and high and low price anomalies. This information is displayed using three different bars: the central moving average (main/middle line), the outer bands (upper and lower lines), and the bandwidth (space between the bands).

The central moving average, or the middle line, is used to display the moving average of the market price. This line essentially displays a smoothed version of the market price, meaning it reflects the current average, and not each individual price change. It is incredibly useful in helping to decipher the general directional trend of the market. The "period" refers to the averaging window. For example, a twenty period main line averages over the previous twenty bars (also known as candles) in the chart. Using a higher number for your period will result in less detail portrayed by this line, as it will be averaged out over a larger amount of price changes.

The upper and lower bands, portrayed in this indicator as the outer lines, expand on the idea of the moving average. These bands run symmetrically, and the central moving average line always runs the equivalent distance between the upper band line as it does the lower band line. The space between the main line and the upper band, and the main line and lower band, is called "standard deviation". They work simultaneously with the bandwidth to indicate the price extremes of the market, or how far the price is straying from its average. These lines represent the markets extreme highs and lows.

The bandwidth represents the distance between the upper and lower bands, and is used to measure the markets volatility. The more choppy the price action of the market is, the greater the bandwidth will be.

The size or distance of the bandwidth correlates with the standard deviation, which is essentially just a measurement of the space between the upper and lower bands, or the sum of the standard deviation. This part of the indicator is useful for recognizing periods of decreasing or increasing market volatility.

Long Order (Purchasing) Entry Overview:
You will want to use the price bars and lower Bollinger band line to help determine when to open a long order form. When the bars meet the lower band line, you

have achieved the first condition necessary for opening a long order. Before you open it, however, you will also want to see the bars retract back towards the main line. This action shows that a brief pullback is taking place after a short-term market peak overbought state.

Short Order (Selling) Entry Overview:
Prior to opening a short order form, you will want to see a few things happen with the Bollinger band lines. Basically what you are looking for is the opposite of what happened when you prepared to open your long order form. You first want to see the bars meet the upper band line, and then they should regress back towards the main line. When this action happens, you are ready to open a short order form.

Step By Step Instructions:
1. Start your trade by opening a One-Minute or Five-Minute time chart. It doesn't matter which one you use, though a Five-Minute chart may be best if you are new to this strategy, or to scalping in general.

2. Set your indicator to the Bollinger band. You will want to use a real time input as well, as the Bollinger band indicator is slightly delayed and can inhibit the accuracy of your trades if it is used on its own. Real time indicators will help give you final proof as to whether or not it is a good idea to enter the market.

3. When opening orders, you will want to set your stop-losses to be no greater than half the width of the Bollinger band. This means that if the total bandwidth is 20 pips, you will want to place the stop-loss at 10 pips.

4. Your take-profit will also be based on the market volatility, generally placed around 5% of the total bandwidth. This is usually 1-6 pips, but this can vary depending on how choppy the market is, so use your discretion.

5. To place long order (purchasing) forms:
   - First, wait until the price bars reach the lower Bollinger band line.
   - From there, they should start to retract back towards the main line.
   - When these two things happen, refer to your real time indicator to ensure the market is still moving in the right direction. If it is, open your long buy order.

6. To place short order (selling) forms:
   - First, wait until the bars reach the upper Bollinger band line.
   - Once they do, they should start to regress back towards the main line.
   - When these two conditions are met, take a look at your real time indicator to ensure the market is still moving in the right direction for your trade. If it is, open your short buy order.

Tips:

- This system works best in a range bound market, therefore it is advisable to use a range finding tool to minimize or prevent you from conducting trades in trending markets. Having a secondary chart with a larger time frame opened with these indicators implemented can help you confirm the current market price is working the way you want it to.

- You will want to use no more than one lot per $10 thousand shares, so the exposure is fairly low.

- Expanding on the last tip: do not use high leverage, as this is a low yielding strategy. Using higher leverages could result in major profit losses.

- The Meta Scalper strategy leaves rarely more than about 10 potential trades per day with the required market entry signals. Because of this, you should be aware that the profits you will make are low, yet consistent.

- The Bollinger band indicator is a delayed indicator, so it is a good idea to use a real time input to help increase the accuracy of your trades.

- You can open a longer time chart on the side to help keep an eye on the market trends, which can also further increase the accuracy of your trades.

Chapter 4: MACD Indicator

The Moving Average Convergence Divergence (MACD) Indicator strategy has the ability to produce over 80% in winning trades if used correctly. The MACD indicator is an incredibly easy one to master, and can be a wonderful tool in scalping. Many traders fail to recognize the benefit of this indicator, so it is often overlooked in trading programs. For those who become fluent in it, they consider it to be one of the most reliable of all existing indicators, if used properly. This section will discuss its purpose and how to use it to maximize your profits.

The MACD indicator was originally developed by Gerald Appel. The indicator consists of two moving averages and a histogram. The averages are deciphered with two different colors: blue to represent the short period average, and red to represent the long period average. The histogram, or the blue bars seen beneath the averages, symbolize the difference between the two averages. The histogram "zero" level is the most important, as it helps indicate a neutral market. From there, we will determine whether the market is on an uptrend or downtrend. When the histogram is above zero level and continuing to incline, the market is on an uptrend. However, when it is below zero, and continuing to decline, the market is on a downtrend.

The histogram is the most important aspect of the MACD indicator. This is the portion we will monitor as our first clue for when the market is in a good position for us to enter. It is important you learn how to monitor the histogram, as it will be critical in your success using this strategy. Mastering this indicator can maximize your scalping profits.

Indicators Used:

As you may have already guessed, you will be using the Moving Average Convergence Divergence (MACD) indicator for this scalping method. This indicator will be your initial determining factor for making decisions in your trading procedures. Additionally, you will be using the Slow Stochastic indicator. The Slow Stochastic indicator has two important levels that will help you confirm your exact entry points. These levels are 80 and 20. Level 80 translates to a market that is overbought, whereas 20 represents a market that has been oversold. Once your MACD histogram expresses your desired trend, you will want to keep a close eye on the Slow Stochastic indicator to finalize your decisions. Typically, when the Stochastic indicator reaches level 80, it will start to decline again, rapidly. Alternatively, when the indicator plummets to level 20, we will likely see it spike back upward again fairly quickly.

Long Order (Purchasing) Entry Overview:

Before placing a long order, you will want to see the histogram well above zero level. First, it should incline, but then it should start to decline back towards zero. Before it reaches zero, however, it should start climbing back up again. This trend indicates that the market is on a reliable uptrend, meaning you should be prepared to start planning your exact long order (purchasing) entry position.

Short Order (Selling) Entry Overview:

Before you place short orders, you will want to see the histogram well below zero level. From its position there, it should start rising back up towards zero. Once it nears zero, you want it to start to decline again, indicating that the market is on a reliable downtrend. During these downtrends is when you will want to start considering your exact short order (selling) entry position.

Step By Step Instructions:

To place long order (purchasing) forms:

1. To begin your trading using the MACD Indicator strategy, you will want to keep an eye on the MACD histogram. When the blue bars are above zero level, you need to start paying attention to find the following trend: first, the histogram should reach high above zero level. From there, they should start returning back down, but should turn around

and start inclining again. This is when you will want to pay careful attention, as this is the first step towards determining your long order entry position.

2. Once your histogram trend matches the above criteria, you will want to take a look at the Stochastic indicator and discover its position. You want it to reach the oversold area (around level 20) before you choose to enter. When the two lines cross each other, and directed upwards, you are almost ready to enter the market.

3. Finally, you are ready to determine your exact entry point. To determine this: keep an eye for the above conditions. Then, when the histogram starts to rise again, and the Stochastic indicator decreases into the oversold zone, you will wait for the candlestick that established this condition to close. As soon as it is closed, you can enter the trade.

4. Once you have entered the trade, you will want to place your stop-losses. For long orders, place them 1 pip below the base candlestick, which is the candlestick where all of the conditions were met and the trade as entered. From here, you will close

your trade in two parts: initially 80% will be closed, and then the last 20% will be closed. Here's how you will want to do it:

- For the 80%: You should have a goal profit target of a 1:1 ratio between stop-losses and take-profits. So, if you risk 25 pips for your stop-losses, your take-profit goal should be 25 pips. When the price reaches your first take-profit goal, you are ready to close the first 80% of your trade.

- For the 20%: You want to move your stop-losses to breakeven, meaning you will place them at the trade's opening value. Your second profit target will be twice what it was for the first 80%. So, if your previous take-profit goal was 25 pips, your second take-profit goal should be 50 pips. Once this value has been met, you can close the remaining 20% of your trade.

To place short order (selling) forms:

1. You will want to start your short order (selling) trades by assessing the MACD histogram, just like you did when you were entering long orders. However, unlike last time, you will want to see the histogram below zero level before you begin to consider an entry point. Once the blue bars reach below zero level, wait for them to start coming back up. Then, they should turn back down again, signifying that the market is on a reliable decline. This will be your first cue for beginning to plot your short order entry.

2. After the MACD histogram trend is desirable, you want to take a look at the Stochastic indicator and see what it is doing. For short orders, you will want the indicator to reach the overbought area, around level 80. When these two lines cross each other and start to head downward, you are almost ready to start your short order entry.

3. Now, to determine your exact entry point, you will want to see the histogram fall again. As soon as that happens, and the Stochastic reaches the overbought area, you want to wait for the

candlestick that established this condition to close. As soon as it closes, you are ready to enter the market with a short trade.

4. Once you have entered the trade, you will want to add the spread to the stop-loss in a short trade, so place the stop-loss 1 pip spread above the high of your base candle stick. Remember, your base candlestick is the one where all of your conditions were met and you entered the market.

5. From here, you will close your trade in two parts: the first 80% and then the remaining 20%.
    - For the 80%: You want a 1:1 stop-loss to take-profit ratio. So, if you risk 25 pips, your take-profit goal should be 25 pips. When the price reaches your take-profit goal, you will close the first 80% of your trade.
    - For the 20%: You want to adjust your stop-loss to breakeven. This means you will move it to the trade's opening value. Then, you will want to change your taken-profit goal. This time, it should be double what last times goal was. So, if your previous goal was 25 pips, your current goal should be 50 pips. Once this goal is reached, you can close the final 20% of your trade.

Tips:

- If you are trying to decide when to enter the market, you want to make sure that you enter at the right time. The histogram trend should be *exactly* as outlined above. So, if your histogram bar is above zero, then drops <u>below</u> zero level but does not come back up, do not enter the trade. However, if after just one bar below zero it starts to incline again, it is safe to enter a long order. Alternatively, if it is below zero level and inclines above zero level but does not return below zero again, do not enter the trade. However, if it rises above zero level for just one bar, then returns below again, you are safe to enter the short order trade. It is important that this cross for zero level for either trade scenario lasts only one bar. If it lasts two or more, the market trend is not reliable and may result in losses instead of gains.
- If you are using MetaTraders, your MACD indicator may appear different than described here. The MetaTrader build-in MACD is a variation of the classic MACD indicator which can be found in Pips Carrier.

Chapter 5: Short Momentum Scalper

The Forex market moves at an incredibly rapid pace. This Short Momentum scalping strategy can be utilized to assist you in focusing on, and entering trades during the stronger short-term trends that may be available depending on the current market. The key to succeeding with this strategy is to be relaxed and make your decisions mindfully and confidently. Short term trading can sometimes be difficult to master, as there is significantly less information available over a short time period than there is over a longer one. Remember: if you are unsure about an entry decision, it is perfectly fine to wait until the next trading opportunity. It is actually better to sit a trade out and develop a better understanding of the market and become confident in your decisions before placing any entry positions, than it is to incur a major loss due to a move you made when you were unconfident in your decision to enter.

Before you choose to proceed with this strategy, you will need to take a look at hourly charts. The hourly chart will be an important technical analysis technique for this strategy, so make sure you take a minute to familiarize yourself with it. When you're scouting the hourly trend, you will be using two Exponential Moving Average (EMA) indicators to help you gain better insight on the current market. The Fast Moving 8 speed and Slow Moving 34 speed EMA's are the best for spotting these trends, so you will want to implement these on your hourly chart. Before moving forward with your trades, you will want to look for certain market trends, which have been described in further detail below. By trying to find where the strongest trends live, and executing your trades during those trends, you will ensure you are entering positions during the best possible time, and minimize your exposure to risks of loss.

Indicators Used:

As previously mentioned, the Short Momentum Scalper strategy will require you to use an hourly chart for your technical analysis. You will need this chart to be equipped with the 8 period and 34 period EMA indicators. You will also have a 5-minute chart open which you will use to conduct each trade. On this one, you will only use the 8 period EMA indicator, the 34 period EMA won't be needed here. The 8 period EMA indicator along with the price bars will help you determine your exact entry points for both long and short orders.

Long Order (Purchasing) Entry Overview

To open a long order form, you will want to see a certain trend take place on the hourly chart. This trend will show the 8 period EMA line cross over the 34 period EMA line, and the market price will rise above both of the EMA's. When this happens, you will then look to the 5-minute chart. There, you want to see the price cross over the 8 period EMA line. When this happens, you are ready to open a long order form. Every time the price crosses the 8 period EMA line on the 5-minute chart, you can open more orders if you choose to. This is one of the customizable features of this strategy, which increases your exposure. This can heighten your risk, but also increase your profit potential. Use stop-losses and take-profits to avoid any major losses when you're opening orders.

Short Order (Selling) Entry Overview

When you're preparing for your short order entry positions, you will be looking for the exact opposite conditions as you were for the long order entries. Here, you want to see the 8 period EMA drop below the 34 period EMA, and the price should drop below both. When this happens, you are ready to move over to the 5 minute chart and prepare to find your exact short order entry position. In this chart, you will want to see the price drop below the 8 period EMA line. Once you see this, you can open your short order entry form. Every time the price crosses below the 8 period EMA, you can open more short orders if you desire. As I said in the last section, always use your stop-losses and take-profits to avoid any major losses with your trades.

Step by Step Instructions

1. Start by opening an hourly chart time. On this chart, you will use the Exponential Moving Average (EMA) indicator in both the Fast Moving Average 8 period and the Slow Moving Average 34 period.
2. Next, open a 5-minute time chart. You will implement an 8 period EMA on this chart as well. You won't need the 34 period on this one.

3. <u>To place long order (purchasing) forms:</u>
    - Look at the hourly chart. When the 8 period EMA is above the 34 period EMA, and the overall market price is above both, you can look over to the 5-minute time chart.
    - On the 5-minute chart, you want to see the market price cross above the 8 period EMA. Once this happens, you can open a long order.
    - On your order, make sure you place a stop-loss at the previous swing-low, to avoid enduring any major losses if the market changes unexpectedly.
    - Place your take-profit at a 1:2 loss to profit ratio on the order. So, if your stop-loss was at 5 pips below the trades entry price, your take-profit will be at 10 pips above.

4. To conduct a short order:
   - Look at the hourly chart time. When the 8 period EMA crosses below the 34 period EMA, and the overall market price is below both, you can return your attention to your 5-minute time chart.
   - On the 5-minute chart, you want to see the overall price drop below the 8 period EMA. When this happens, you can safely open a short order.
   - Ensure you place a stop-loss at the previous swing-high to prevent you from risking any major losses.
   - Again, place your take-profit at a 1:2 loss to profit ratio on the short order. So, if your stop-loss was at 5 pips above the trades entry price, your take-profit will be at 10 pips below.

Tips

- It is important that you use the hourly chart for your technical analysis, to help you make informed decisions as to when you should open each position. This will help improve accuracy, minimize risk, and increase your chances of profit.

- If you desire, you can open multiple long orders and multiple short orders during each swing process, to increase exposure and potential profitability. Make sure to always use your stop-losses to prevent any major profit losses.

Chapter 6: About Options

The Options market is considerably different than the forex market. While the primary idea behind scalping the market remains consistent between the two, the market itself and the way it is worked is drastically different from one to the other. While Forex trades are instantaneous, Option trades are not, in a sense. Each time you place an order (called a call or a put in the Options market) you are actually opening a contract that gives you the right to buy or sell an underlying asset at a specific price either on or before a predetermined date. Please take note that I said the *right* to the buying and selling of the underlying asset, and not the *obligation*. You can choose to abandon the contract if you desire, without acting on it. However, if the conditions are right and you wish to, you can proceed with the purchasing process and fulfill the contract. This contract must be fulfilled within' a set amount of time, as option contracts can expire, thus turning them invalid. Also, unlike Forex, the options market closes and opens, so you will be required to wait for the market to open in the morning before you can start any trades.

Chapter 7: Gamma Scalping

Gamma scalping refers to the process where you as the trader will adjust the deltas of a long option premium and long gamma portfolio of options as an attempt to scalp enough money from each contract to offset the time decay of the position. Offsetting the theta (described below) and conducting trades in a quicker time frame are the primary purposes behind the gamma scalping strategy.

Gamma scalping is an options trading strategy that is completely non-directional. That means that even back-and-forth movements in the market can result in profits for you as a trader, sometimes even big ones. This strategy may not be for everyone, however it is essential for everyone to understand. The importance of understanding this system lies in the fact that gamma scalping is a substantial element in the machine that prices market volatility. It still has the ability to be extremely profitable as well, if users educate themselves and learn to use it properly. This strategy is best suited for individuals who are well versed and possess experience with the trading markets, but can be mastered by anyone who is willing to learn. To understand the process of this scalping strategy, you must first understand how options traders trade using "the greeks".

The metrics that are used to measure the affect of the influences of an option's value are referred to as the greeks. These metrics provide crucial information for the underlying asset price, time and market volatility. Each influence is assigned its own metric, which are named using the greek alphabet, hence the term "the greeks". These metrics include: delta, gamma, theta and vega. You will need to develop an understanding for each of these metrics, as they are the indicators you will use with the gamma scalping method. Below, I will explain each one in detail and provide examples to help you develop your understanding.

Indicators Used:

The indicators you will pay attention to for this strategy are elements that are relevant to all options-based trades. Since they can be a little confusing, especially to someone who doesn't know what they're looking at, I have provided some details and examples of each metric below.

Delta

The delta metric directly refers to the option value's rate of change in relation to a change in the underlying asset, in which shares are being purchased and sold. Deltas are expressed as a perfect and recorded in decimal form. "Calls" (the option to buy) have positive deltas, "puts" (the option to sell) have negative deltas.

> *Example:* If an options delta is 0.40, this means it moves 40% as much as the underlying stock. If it rises by one dollar, then the 0.40 delta will rise by 40 cents. You can think of your delta as a representation of how many shares of the underlying stock you have the right to. Imagine you have a call that represents your right to 100 shares. If that call has a 0.40 delta, it will move 40% as much as the underlying stock does. It

also means that you have the right to 40 shares of the underlying stock that you are trading.

The term "at-the-money" refers to a situation where both the call and put options are simultaneously at the money, or at about a 0.50 delta (50%). The terms "in-the-money" and "out-of-the-money" then would both refer to how high or low the delta is. If an option is in-the-money, this means that it has a greater delta that is anywhere above 0.50 all the way up to 1.00 (100%). Alternatively, if an option is out-of-the-money, then it has a lower delta that is anywhere lower than 0.50, all the way down to 0 (0%).

<u>Gamma</u>
The gamma metric represents the option deltas rate of change in direct relation to any alterations in the underlying asset.

As explained previously, the more in-the-money an option is, the larger the delta. Similarly, the more out-of-the-money the option is, the smaller its delta. As the price of the underlying stock changes, the more in- or out-of-the-money the option becomes, therefore putting the delta in a constant state of change.

Occasionally, these changes can have a significant impact on your profit and loss (P&L). It is crucial to understand how diversity in the delta will affect your P&L, thus making gamma an important metric to monitor.

Gamma is recorded similar to deltas, and represents how many deltas an option has. This means that if the options gamma is 0.15, then the option will earn 0.15 deltas whenever the underlying stock increase, and lose 0.15 deltas when the underlying stock decreases.

Long options (both calls and puts) possess positive gamma. Short options (both calls and puts) have negative gamma. Positive gamma assists you, leading to you gaining more on your wins and losing less on your losses than the delta would indicate. Negative gamma is damaging to your profit.

Theta

Theta expresses the change to an options value in relation to any changes in the time until its expiration.

The more that time passes, the less an option is worth. Therefore, theta is a metric that represents how much value an option will lose on each passing day. The theta metric is recorded in dollars and cents. An option that possesses a theta of 0.07 loses seven cents on every passing day, as a result of time decay.

Long options hold a negative theta, meaning they lose money as time passes. Short options carry a positive theta, meaning they actually gain money as time passes.

Theta and gamma are opposites, and counter each other depending on the conditions of an option. The benefit held by long options due to having a positive gamma is countered by the loss incurred by negative theta. Conversely, the benefit of a short option having a positive theta is countered by the loss acquired by the negative gamma.

Vega

Vega portrays any changes to the options value in direct relation to a change in the implied volatility of the option.

Implied volatility refers to the volatile component embedded in an options price. The option price closely follows the implied volatility: if the options implied volatility is high, the price will be too. However, if the options implied volatility is low, then the price will also be low. Implied volatility can change, and the vega metric is used to represent the extent to which these changes will affect the value of the option.

Like theta, vega is recorded in dollars and cents. So, if an option possesses a vega of 0.03, it will earn three cents every time there is a one-point rise in implied volatility, and it will lose three cents every time there is a one-point fall in the implied volatility.

Entry Overview:

When you are preparing to gamma scalp, you will want to create a delta-neutral trade position. You will do this by offsetting the deltas by selling stock every time you place an option trade. So, if you buy shares in the market, you will want to sell an equal amount in order to offset the immediate directional sensitivity. Creating this delta neutral position means you will be close to 0.50 delta, or at-the-money.

Step By Step Instructions:

1. Create a delta-neutral position. To do this, you will want to sell an amount of short shares that will equal the amount of long shares you opened. For example, if you buy 100 ABC calls that each have a 0.40 delta, your position delta would be 40. This is the equivalent of 4000 shares (delta x number of shares you bought).

2. As the stock rises and falls, your delta will change due to gamma. The gamma will benefit your trade, and the delta will change in your favour. The delta will get shorter as your underlying stock falls and longer as it rises. As the delta recalibrates, you will develop an

opportunity: hedge your investment as your delta changes, which will result in scalping the stock.

- Hedging your investments means to continue making investments for the benefit of previous ones made, so:
- When the stock falls and the delta gets short, you will buy stock.
- When the stock rises and the delta becomes long, you can sell stock.
- These scalping transactions create cash flow through the method of "buy low, sell high".

3. You want to beware of the theta in your scalping procedures. You might recall that the theta is the amount of money stock loses every day. In order to counter this loss, you will need to scalp *more* than the theta will cost. (So, if the theta is 0.04 per call, on 100 contracts that is 4.00. Thats $400 worth of cash per day. You will need to make more than $400 in order to see profits.)
    - Remember that theta is a metric that measures implied volatility. If an options theta is high, you will be required to scalp more for profit in order to cover the higher theta value. Likewise, if the

options theta is low, you will only need to scalp a lower amount in order to cover the lower theta value. Keep this in mind when placing trades to help you maximize your profit potential.

Conclusion

Thank you again for downloading this book!

I hope *Scalping Trading Top 5 Strategies: Making Money With* was able to help you develop an understanding of scalping and how to turn it into a profitable trading strategy.

The next step is to enter the Forex or Options market and practice the strategies we've discussed, and start earning money!

Finally, if you've enjoyed this book, please take the time to share your thoughts and post a review on Amazon. It'd be greatly appreciated!

Thank you and good luck!

Glossary

Averaging Out

This strategy refers to spreading your trades over a large number of less expensive stocks in order to reduce the overall risk. The idea is that you will only incur a small risk to each individual stock, rather than one large risk on one large amount of stock.

Bars (AKA Candlesticks)

These bars graphs represent the current market price. They are constantly moving as the market price changes.

Bollingers Band

A form of volatility indicator that consists of three primary lines and uses three different indication techniques to provide information on the current market. The upper and lower band lines represent the markets recent highs and lows, the middle represents the moving average, and the bandwidth (space between upper and lower lines) represents the markets current volatility.

Exponential Moving Average

A form of moving average that carries more weight in its latest data than other moving averages do. This form of moving average reacts much quicker to recent price changes than others, such as a simple moving average, do.

The Greeks

Metrics that are used to determine the current market action in options trading. The Greeks include delta, gamma, theta and vega, and each represent a specific aspect of the market. They act as indicators in the options market, and are relevant to every single trade. You do not implement them, they simply exist.

Long Order:

The order which correlates with the purchasing process of a trade. Long orders are placed before short orders.

Moving Average

A type of technical analysis used to help smooth out the price action. This type of indicator has a line that will follow the market prices general direction without all the choppy action of each individual price change in the market, which you would see in the bars.

Moving Average Convergence Divergence

A form of trading indicator that is used to reveal the changes in: strength, direction, momentum and duration of a trend in a stock's price.

Range Bound

A strategy that identifies stocks that are trading in channels. Through technical analysis, you can find major support and resistance levels and use these to assist you in making buy/sell decisions. A trend trader will buy stock at the bottom of the channel (the lower level of support) and sell them at the top of the channel (near the resistance).

Short Order:

The order relating to the selling process of a trade. Short orders are placed after long orders and, in this case, complete the scalping process and result in your profit.

Stochastic Oscillator

As a form of technical analysis, these are a momentum indicator that use support and resistance levels. The term stochastic refers to the location of a current price in the market, in relation to its range of price over a set period of time. The term oscillator refers to a device used to convey the momentum and direction of the market, based on its recent history.

Stop-Loss:

An order that is opened at the same time as a long or short order, and minimizes the risk of losses associated with a trade. For example, if your stock is worth $50, and you place a stop loss at $49, then if the market value drops to $49, the stop loss will trigger a sale at the next available market price. If this is $48.80, then your stock will sell for $48.80.

Take-Profit:

The opposite of a stop-loss, a take-profit is an order that is also opened at the same time as a long or short order. It encourages a sale in the other direction, resulting in profit for you and is used to reduce your risk of the market value dropping before you make your sale. For example, if your stock is worth $50 at the trades entry, and you set a take-profit at $55, then when the market value hits $55, your take-profit will trigger a sale at the next available price. If this value is $55.10, then your stock will sell at $55.10. Take-profits can also be regarded as profit goals on each individual trade.

www.ingramcontent.com/pod-product-compliance
Lightning Source LLC
Chambersburg PA
CBHW070356190526
45169CB00003B/1033